GO FACTS NATURAL DISASTERS

Wild Weather

A & C BLACK • LONDON

Wild Weather

contents

© Blake Publishing 2006
Additional material © A & C Black Publishers Ltd 2006

First published in Australia in 2006 by Blake Education Pty Ltd

This edition published in the United Kingdom in 2006 by
A & C Black Publishers Ltd, 38 Soho Square, London W1D 3HB
www.acblack.com

Hardback edition
ISBN-10: 0-7136-7958-1
ISBN-13: 978-0-7136-7958-8

Paperback edition
ISBN-10: 0-7136-7966-2
ISBN-13: 978-0-7136-7966-3

A CIP record for this book is available from the British Library.

Written by Ian Rohr
Publisher: Katy Pike
Editor: Paul O'Beirne
Design and layout by The Modern Art Production Group

Photo credits: p5 (br), p7 (bl), p9 (bl), p10 (tl), p11 (tl, tr, br), p13 (middle - br,
bottom - bl), p19 (tr), p21 (bl), p25 (tr, br), p27 (tl, bl), p29 (tr) (australian picture
library); pp16–17 (Paul McEvoy).

Printed in China by WKT Company Ltd.

This book is produced using paper that is made from wood grown in managed,
sustainable forests. It is natural, renewable and recyclable. The logging and
manufacturing processes conform to the environmental regulations of the country
of origin.

What is a Tropical Cyclone?

Tropical cyclones are enormous circular storms. They form over the warm waters of the tropics and mainly affect coastal regions and islands.

Tropical cyclones consist of **torrential** rains and winds of up to 300 km/h (186 mph) swirling around a central **eye**. They can grow to a massive size but are usually 200–500 km (125-310 miles) in diameter. They can travel hundreds of kilometres in a single day.

A cyclone is a hurricane is a typhoon

They have different names, but cyclones, hurricanes and typhoons are all the same weather feature. They are called cyclones in Australia and India, typhoons in Japan and hurricanes in the UK and America. **Collectively** they are known as tropical cyclones. Most tropical cyclones are given people's names, such as Cyclone Tracy, or Hurricane Katrina.

Cyclones and us

Up to 80 tropical cyclones form each year. Many stay out at sea, where they cause little damage. When tropical cyclones reach land they are very destructive. They destroy buildings, cause massive flooding, ruin crops and kill many people.

Once they reach land, tropical cyclones rapidly die out, because they can no longer gain the energy they need from the warm, humid air over the ocean. This is also why tropical cyclones cannot form over land.

Category	Winds	Typical effects
1	Gusts less than 125 km/h (78 mph).	Damage to some crops, trees and caravans.
2	Gusts 125–170 km/h (78–106 mph).	Minor house damage. Significant damage to signs, trees and caravans. Heavy damage to some crops. Risk of power failure.
3	Gusts 170–225 km/h (106–140 mph).	Some roof and structural damage. Some caravans destroyed. Power failure likely.
4	Gusts 225–280 km/h (140–174 mph).	Significant roofing loss and structural damage. Many caravans destroyed. Dangerous flying **debris**. Widespread power failure.
5	Gusts more than 280 km/h (174 mph).	Extremely dangerous with widespread destruction.

Tropical cyclones are the most powerful storms on Earth.

Modern technology gives us detailed warnings that were impossible a century ago. Satellites can tell us how big hurricanes are and **track** their movements; while storm-penetrating aircraft can tell us how fast they are moving.

GO FACT!

DID YOU KNOW?

The 1970 Bhola cyclone in Bangladesh was the deadliest cyclone ever recorded. The winds and a **storm surge** killed at least 300 000 people.

How do Tropical Cyclones Form?

The energy that leads to tropical cyclones comes from the Sun. Cyclones form over warm water, where wind and rising moist air combine.

A cyclone is born

Tropical areas receive more sunlight than anywhere else on Earth, so air and water temperatures are much warmer. Hurricanes can only form when the ocean water is 26.5°C or higher. The warm water heats the air above it. The warm, moist air rises quickly as water **vapour** to form storm clouds.

The eye of the cyclone

The exchange of heat from the water's surface to the atmosphere creates wind. The rotation of the Earth means that the rising air forms a spinning column. As the cyclone grows, air continues to be sucked into the **low pressure** centre. The wind builds up more speed, eventually circling the eye that develops in the cyclone's centre. The eye is the area of lowest pressure and is a calm and virtually windless place, despite the chaos surrounding it. The area immediately surrounding the eye is called the **eye wall**. It is here that the fastest and most destructive winds are found.

About 2 billion tonnes of moisture are picked up and released by a hurricane each day.

The winds of a tropical cyclone rotate clockwise in the Southern Hemisphere and anticlockwise in the Northern Hemisphere.

Storm surges cause 90% of all hurricane-related deaths. These waves can rise 7.5 metres above the ocean's surface.

GO FACT!

DID YOU KNOW?
Tropical cyclones begin to die out once they reach land because they need the warm, humid air over the ocean to provide energy.

7

Predicting and Tracking Tropical Cyclones

Meteorologists study the weather and try to predict what it will do. Meteorologists study tropical cyclones as they form to give forecasts about the likely path of the storm.

Tools of the trade

Meteorologists use a range of tools to predict and track tropical cyclones. These include observations, **analysis**, **computer models** and even flying into the middle of cyclones.

Developing cyclones are observed using satellites, **buoys**, **radar** and aircraft. Many accurate observations need to be made. Once collected, the **data** is fed into a range of computer models, which make millions of calculations to produce information on the cyclone's likely growth and direction.

Hit and miss

A meteorologist studies the behaviour of past cyclones to help predict the intensity and path of future storms. Weather systems are highly complex, making them difficult to predict. Despite recent improvements in computer modelling, cyclone predictions can be inaccurate.

Meteorologists also need to be highly skilled interpreters of data. Computer models require massive amounts of data which take long periods of time to process. Models can only be run a few times each day, giving the cyclone time to change intensity and direction.

A range of computer models is used, and each one may give different results. When this occurs, the meteorologists must determine which model is the most likely to be accurate under the circumstances.

Ships also send in weather reports. This information is combined with other sources to give a clearer picture of how the cyclone may develop.

The emergency plan for a Category 2 cyclone is the same as for a Category 3 cyclone. This allows for a margin of error.

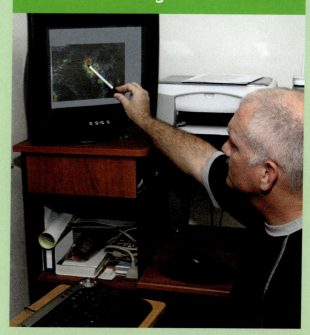

Planes that take meteorologists and recording equipment into the centre of cyclones are called 'hurricane hunters'.

GO FACT!

DID YOU KNOW?

Scientists try to predict natural disasters to limit the loss of life and property. The United Nations estimates that natural disasters have killed 1 500 000 people over the last 20 years – 94% by tropical cyclones, floods, droughts and earthquakes.

Case Study – Hurricane Katrina

On August 28th 2005, the Mayor of New Orleans ordered the total evacuation of the city. Hurricane Katrina hit New Orleans the next day. It killed 1418 people, with a damage bill over $200 billion (£106 billion).

Katrina hits land

Hurricane Katrina hit on August 29th as a Category 4 storm. It created havoc in the states of Mississippi and Alabama, but New Orleans, Louisiana was the worst hit. Winds of 160 km/h (100 mph) tore roofs from buildings, cut power lines, **felled** trees and wrecked thousands of shops and cars.

After Katrina

A **levee system** protected New Orleans from Lake Pontchartrain. Part of it was **breached** by Katrina. Flood waters from the lake poured into New Orleans and 80% of the city flooded. People were stranded on roofs and thousands took refuge in the city's Superdome stadium.

One hundred thousand people remained in the city. Food and water ran out as authorities were unable to cope with the sheer devastation caused by the storm. On August 31st, the Mayor again ordered the full **evacuation** of the city.

In the largest airlift in US history thousands of survivors were flown to neighbouring states. The city was left deserted as the authorities began the massive clean-up operation.

Hurricane Katrina is the most expensive natural disaster ever to have hit the United States of America.

Over one million people were displaced by the disaster and five million were left without power.

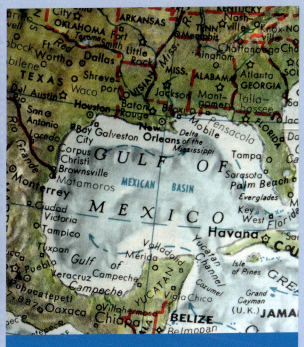

An area almost as large as the United Kingdom was affected by Katrina.

GO FACT!

DID YOU KNOW?

New Orleans sits 2 metres below sea level. Its levee system was built to withstand a Category 3 storm.

What to do in a Cyclone

When it becomes clear that a cyclone is going to hit a populated area, all people can do is follow some basic rules.

Tropical cyclone survival guide

1. Before the cyclone season

- Check that the roof, gutters and eaves are secure.
- Trim overhanging tree branches away from the house.
- Fit windows with shutters or screens.
- Clear up the garden and store loose materials.
- Prepare an emergency kit.
- Prepare a list of emergency telephone numbers.

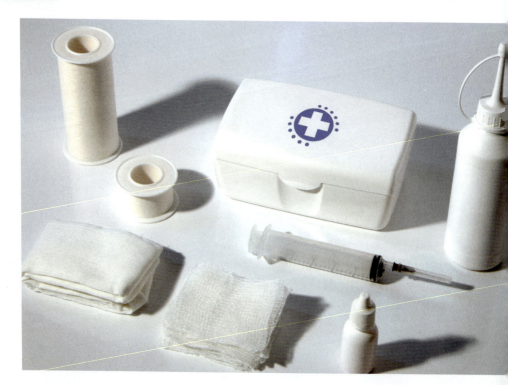

2. When a cyclone warning is issued

- Put loose items inside the house.
- Put outdoor furniture away.
- Fill rubbish bins with water.
- Fill the car with fuel and put it under cover if possible.
- Close shutters or board/tape up windows.
- Pack an evacuation kit that includes warm clothes, essential medicines, valuables, important documents, photos and the emergency kit.
- Listen to local television/radio news for updates.

3. During the cyclone

- Disconnect electrical appliances and turn off the gas.
- Stay inside in the strongest part of the house (cellar, hall, etc.) and keep away from windows.
- Protect yourself with mattresses, blankets, rugs, etc. if the building starts to break apart.
- Listen to the radio for updates.
- Remember that the eye of the cyclone may make it seem that the danger is over but strong winds will probably resume from the opposite direction.
- If you are driving, pull over and park. Stay away from beaches, low lying land, trees, power lines, creeks and rivers. Stay in the vehicle.

4. After the cyclone

- Do not go outside until there is an official 'all clear'.
- Check for gas leaks. Do not use wet electrical equipment.
- Beware of fallen power lines and damaged trees, buildings, etc.
- Take note of all official warnings.
- Do not use the telephone unnecessarily.

Tornadoes

Tornadoes, also called twisters, are revolving funnels of air that stretch from storm clouds to the ground. Tornadoes can suck up anything from cows and cars to barns and combine harvesters.

How do tornadoes form?

Tornadoes form inside giant, **turbulent**, long-lasting thunderstorms, known as supercells. Warm air is drawn up into the storm cloud, spinning around as it rises – similar to water going down a plughole. As the air at the base of the supercell twirls, it forms a funnel shape that can spin down towards the ground. Once this **vortex** of spinning air touches the ground, it officially becomes a tornado.

Generally the wider the base of the tornado, the more destructive it will be. Big tornadoes can generate wind speeds of up to 500 km/h (310 mph).

Where are tornadoes found?

Tornadoes are found in many parts of the world, including Asia, Europe and Australia but most commonly in parts of the United States. The broad, flat plains of the American Midwest are especially prone to tornadoes with about 1000 forming each year. A broad path through the American states of Missouri, Kansas, Oklahoma and Texas is known as 'Tornado Alley' because of the frequency of tornadoes in this area.

The most deadly and destructive tornadoes form in supercell thunderstorms.

Tornadoes act like giant vacuum cleaners and can completely demolish buildings.

A typical tornado is about 300 metres wide and travels at about 50 km/h (30 mph).

GO FACT!

DID YOU KNOW?

The frightening black colour of tornadoes is caused by the debris and dirt they to suck up as soon as they hit the ground.

15

How to Make a Tornado

You wouldn't want a tornado to twist through your kitchen, but this miniature one, using water instead of air, will show you how they work.

What you need:

- two empty 1-litre plastic bottles with the labels removed
- a rubber or metal washer, roughly the same width as the tops of the bottles, with a hole in it
- a roll of electrical or duct tape
- water
- food colouring (optional)

Making your tornado

1 Fill three-quarters of this bottle with water. Add the food colouring.

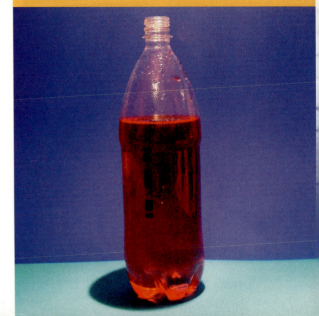

16

2 Tape the washer to the top of the bottle. Do not cover the hole in the washer.

3 Tape the two bottles securely together at the neck.

4 Quickly turn the bottles over and place them on a flat, stable surface.

5 As water swirls down it makes a tornado-shaped funnel. It forms a vortex, just like the air in a tornado.

17

Case Study – Jarrell, Texas

Shortly before 3:45 pm on May 27th 1997, a violent tornado struck the small town of Jarrell. By nightfall, 27 people were dead.

Wild weather warning

Jarrell's tornado alert siren sounded after a group of tornadoes were spotted 2 km (1.2 miles) north of the town. Less than 20 minutes later the twisters had merged into a single tornado 1.2 km (0.7 miles) wide, which bore down on the Double Creek Estate. Though massive, the tornado was slowmoving, and spent the next half-hour destroying areas of Jarrell.

Most of the houses in Double Creek lacked basements, so people sheltered in rooms. The tornado destroyed 45 of the 50 houses in Double Creek, leaving only the concrete slabs. Twenty-seven people died in the tornado.

Force-5

The tornado was given the rare and maximum Force-5 rating, which means that the wind speed was over 417 km/h (260 mph). The tornado pulled asphalt off the roads and killed and maimed livestock. Cars were tossed in the air and a 10-tonne combine harvester was blown across a field. In just half an hour the Jarrell tornado had caused nearly $20 million (£10.5 million) of damage.

Scale	Winds	Typical effects
F0	<116 km/h (72 mph)	Some damage to chimneys, trees and signs.
F1	117–180 km/h (72–112 mph)	Peels surface off roofs. Mobile homes pushed off foundations or overturned. Cars blown off roads.
F2	181–253 km/h (113–157 mph)	Roofs torn off houses. Mobile homes demolished. Large trees snapped or uprooted. Cars lifted off ground.
F3	254–332 km/h (158–206 mph)	Roofs and some walls torn off houses. Trains overturned. Most trees in forest uprooted. Heavy cars lifted off the ground.
F4	333–416 km/h (207–259 mph)	Houses completely destroyed. Structures with weak foundations blown away some distance. Cars and large missiles thrown.
F5	417–509 km/h (260–316 mph)	Houses destroyed and swept away. Large missiles fly through the air in excess of 100 metres. Trees debarked. Incredible phenomena will occur.

Jarrell was largely destroyed by another tornado in May 1989. One woman was killed and 28 people injured. That storm severely damaged or destroyed 35 houses and 12 mobile homes.

Tornadoes aren't ranked until the damage has been inspected. There is no way of measuring a tornado's intensity while it is still active.

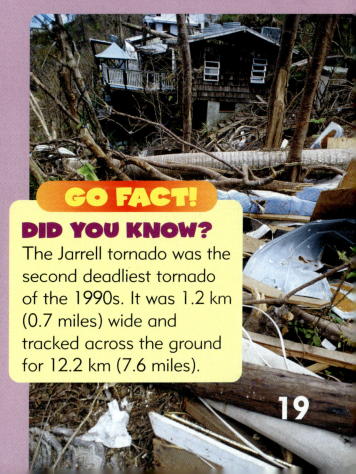

GO FACT!

DID YOU KNOW?

The Jarrell tornado was the second deadliest tornado of the 1990s. It was 1.2 km (0.7 miles) wide and tracked across the ground for 12.2 km (7.6 miles).

I Survived a Tornado!

In Tornado Alley people build underground shelters near their homes. They watch the skies and listen to the radio for warnings during the summer tornado season.

Dear Nan,

Remember how you told me about that tornado years ago? The one that killed 89 people? I've got my own twister tale now!

It all happened at my friend Rick's place. Rick's mum kept listening to the radio and checking the sky, as there were lots of thunderstorms about. As a huge black cloud appeared, the radio gave a tornado warning. As it got closer, a gigantic grey funnel wound out of it towards the ground! As it touched down it changed colour from grey to pitch black. We all quickly piled into the shelter.

At first everything was quiet, but then we heard a noise like a freight train. The trapdoor shook violently, even though two big bolts held it down. It was scary! Then, as quickly as it arrived, it was gone.

Everything was such a mess! The Monroe's car was on its roof. Half the barn roof was gone. We were lucky - a lady was killed when the twister demolished her mobile home.

Keep well!

Love,

Toby

The storm cloud began to form a funnel. Mrs Monroe told us to run for the shelter out back.

Moments later the funnel touches down becoming very black and dark due to the amount of debris it sucked up.

Mrs Monroe was the first to emerge after the storm. We sat in the shelter for about 20 minutes after the tornado was over, just to be sure.

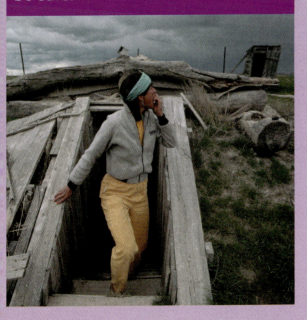

The Monroe's car! If the tornado did this to their car, what would it have done to us if we hadn't been in the shelter? We were lucky — some people had nowhere to hide.

21

What Causes Floods?

Floods occur when water from a river or sea overflows onto nearby land. In heavy, prolonged rain, the ground becomes completely soaked. All the excess rainwater runs into rivers, causing them to rise, overflow and flood the land.

River floods

River floods usually occur after heavy rainfall. It is natural for rivers to flood **periodically**. Rivers are most prone to flooding in areas that have extremes of wet and dry. Some rivers flood during wet seasons and then dwindle, or even totally dry up, when the rains stop. Other rivers flood during warm weather when melting snow and ice fill them to overflowing.

Sea floods

Sea floods are uncommon but tend to be more destructive. They are often caused by events such as storms and tropical cyclones. Sea floods are also caused by strong winds and high tides. If a storm coincides with a high tide, the water can rise way above the usual high-tide mark.

Flash floods

Flash floods can be the most dangerous of all. When they occur in river valleys, walls of water can reach heights of 9 metres. Flash floods are particularly dangerous because they happen with little or no warning. When floodwaters suddenly appear, people, trees, cars and buildings are swept away.

Crossing swollen rivers claims the lives of many people during floods — a depth of 15 centimetres of fast-flowing water is enough to knock a person off their feet. Sixty centimetres of moving water is enough to sweep a car downstream.

In flood-prone areas, such as Inle Lake, Burma, people build their homes on stilts.

Low-lying nations, such as Bangladesh, the Netherlands and some Pacific islands, are at risk from regular sea floods.

GO FACT!

DID YOU KNOW?

Floods cause more damage and kill more people than any other form of wild weather.

Flood Damage and Benefits

Floods are often destructive, but they can also have benefits. Some areas of the world rely on floods to keep their land fertile.

Flood damage

Floods cause enormous damage. Rushing walls of water wash people, animals, buildings and vehicles away. The debris carried along by the floodwaters also causes havoc, battering humans and property. Floods burst sewage pipes and gas mains, causing pollution. They bring down electrical wires, which cause deaths by electrocution.

Floods also destroy agricultural crops. Floodwaters can lead to the spread of deadly, infectious diseases as drinking water becomes polluted.

Flood benefits

Despite this damage, some floods also provide benefits. River floods leave behind large amounts of **sediment**. Sediment is rich in nutrients. Farmers plough the sediment back into the soil in order to grow food crops. In ancient Egypt, the yearly flooding by the Nile River allowed the **arid** land to support people for thousands of years. The Aswan Dam now prevents the Nile River from flooding. Today Egyptian farmers can grow crops but they must use chemical fertilisers to keep the land fertile.

The mud and debris left behind by floods requires massive clean-up efforts.

Like many ancient cities Pagan, in Burma, was built on the fertile soils of a flood plain.

It can take many weeks for floodwaters to drain away.

GO FACT!

DID YOU KNOW?

To the ancient Egyptians the regular flooding of the Nile was a symbol of life.

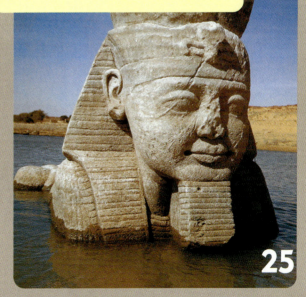

Case Study – Dresden, Germany

In August 2002 heavy rains caused extensive flooding in Europe. One badly affected area was the German city of Dresden, famous for its historic buildings and artworks.

Thursday 15th August

As the Elbe River rose, emergency workers built sandbag walls around Dresden's city centre.

Many of the museums and art galleries held historic artworks in their basements. As water flowed into buildings, such as the Zwinger Palace art museum, volunteers moved the artworks to higher levels. Paintings, too large to move, were hung from basement ceilings. Emergency workers tried to pump the water out.

Friday 16th August

On Friday, workers gave up building walls and pumping, as the floodwaters broke through. The river broke all previous records as it rose above 9 metres. Lower levels of the Zwinger Palace and the railway station were flooded.

Saturday 17th August

The flooding of the Elbe River rose to a 160-year high on Saturday, reaching 9.6 metres. The previous record had been 8.77 metres.

After the flood

Water levels dropped on Sunday. After the floodwaters receded, much of central Dresden was left coated in a layer of thick mud.

Fortunately most of Dresden's artworks were saved from the floodwaters, but damage to buildings was estimated at millions of pounds.

During the floods the Elbe rose from a normal summer level of 2 metres to over 9 metres.

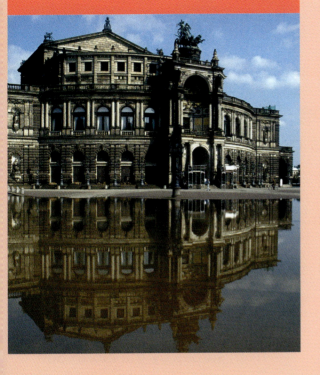

Other European countries affected were the Czech Republic, Austria, Slovakia, Russia and Romania.

GO FACT!

DID YOU KNOW?

The floods caused billions of pounds worth of damage across central and Eastern Europe. Roads, buildings and essential services were damaged. The floods also claimed the lives of over 100 people.

Dresden is known as 'Florence on the Elbe' because, like the Italian city of Florence, it is home to many historic buildings and beautiful artworks.

Preventing Floods

Flood damage can be reduced by building dams, barriers, dykes and levees.

Dams

Dams are concrete walls built across rivers. A **reservoir** of water forms behind the dam. Gates in the wall **regulate** the flow of water downstream. During heavy rain, the dam collects excess water and prevents the flooding of downstream valleys and plains.

However, if a dam bursts, or overflows, it can actually cause floods.

Barriers

Flood barriers and concrete sea walls protect low-lying coastal areas against storm surges and high tides. In England, a moveable flood barrier on the River Thames protects London from surges by the North Sea. The rotating steel gates rise when there is a tidal surge.

Dykes and levees

Dykes are large walls built to hold back the sea. Much of the Netherlands is **reclaimed** land that lies below sea level. The dykes help prevent flooding.

Levees are walls built along river banks. They help to keep water flowing along its normal channel when river levels rise. Levees are made of concrete, or earth and sandbags.

Dams now control the flow of most of the world's major rivers.

Occasionally a dam will burst, leading to huge flooding as a great mass of water is released.

Many of the Netherlands' dykes have been raised and reinforced following disastrous floods in 1953 when 1794 people died due to sea floods.

DID YOU KNOW?

The barriers on the Thames were first used in 1983 and have been raised 25 times since. They are the world's largest moveable flood barriers. London has not flooded since the building of the barriers.

29

Table

Year	Location	Result
Cyclone/ Hurricane 1970	Bangladesh	Considered the worst natural disaster of the 20th century. Over 500 000 people were killed as a result of the cyclone and flooding. Winds of up to 230 km/h (143 mph) slammed into the heavily populated coastal region. The winds caused huge waves which deluged entire villages and left millions homeless.
1998	Honduras and Nicaragua	Hurricane Mitch killed 10 000 and left over two million homeless. Mudslides caused by torrential rain buried thousands more. Disease and famine were still rampant months after the storm.
1992	USA	Hurricane Andrew was the second costliest storm, after Hurricane Katrina, in US history causing $27 billion (£14 billion) worth of damage. Fifty-eight people lost their lives.
Tornado 1925	USA	A tornado ripped through the states of Missouri, Illinois and Indiana leaving behind a trail of death and destruction. It lasted a record $3\frac{1}{2}$ hours killing 695 people and injuring 1980. The tornado peaked in Illinois where it destroyed the town of Gorham, killing half the residents. Its winds clocked at 483 km/h (300 mph).
1989	Bangladesh	Regarded as the deadliest tornado in history, it killed 1300 people and left 50 000 homeless.
Flood 1887	China	Regarded as one fo the worst floods in history, the Huang He (Yellow River) burst its banks in Huayan Kou, killing 900 000 people.
1931	China	This is regarded as the worst natural disaster of all time. Nearly four million people lost their lives when the Huang He River burst its banks. People died from disease, starvation and drowning.
1991	China	Tai Hu, a lake at the mouth of the Yangtze River, engulfed an industrial and agricultural region. The economic loss was devastating, and over 2000 people died. In one province, a million homes were swept away. Overall, the flood affected the lives of 220 million people.

Glossary

analysis examination of something in detail in order to understand it

arid dry country which is usually not good for farming unless irrigation is used

breached made a gap or opening

buoys floats used in waterways to either provide directions or house recording equipment used to monitor waves, etc.

collectively as a whole

computer models models drawn by computers to help understand how something works

cyclone (also hurricane or typhoon) a tropical storm with very strong winds

data information in the form of facts or statistics

debris fragments of things broken down; rubbish

evacuation the process of moving people to a safe place when some form of danger or disaster threatens

eye an area like a hole in the centre of a tropical cyclone

eye wall the part around the eye which has the strongest winds

felled to cut or knock down

levee system a bank built up to prevent a river from overflowing

low pressure air pressure is the weight of the air in the atmosphere pressing down on the Earth. Areas of low pressure are caused by warm air rising from the ground. The weather is more changeable in areas of low pressure and low air pressure often leads to bad weather.

periodically something that occurs or appears once in a while

radar a device used to track the position of things, such as planes and ships, by sending out radio signals that are reflected back from the object and shown on a screen

reclaimed taken back, e.g. land reclaimed from the sea by draining it

regulate to control the way something operates

reservoir a natural or artificial place where water is collected and stored

sediment material such as sand, gravel and clay carried along by water. When the water stops or flows more slowly the sediment sinks.

storm surge a large sudden rise in sea level near the eye of the cyclone; large waves caused by strong winds. If the winds are blowing towards the coast, the resulting storm surges can cause heavy damage.

torrential a very heavy, violent downpour of rain, sometimes lasting for a long period

track to follow the course of something by using radar, etc.

turbulent something that is wild and stormy

vapour a mass of tiny drops of water in the air, which looks like mist

vortex a whirling mass of air, water, flames, etc.

Index